MW01716400

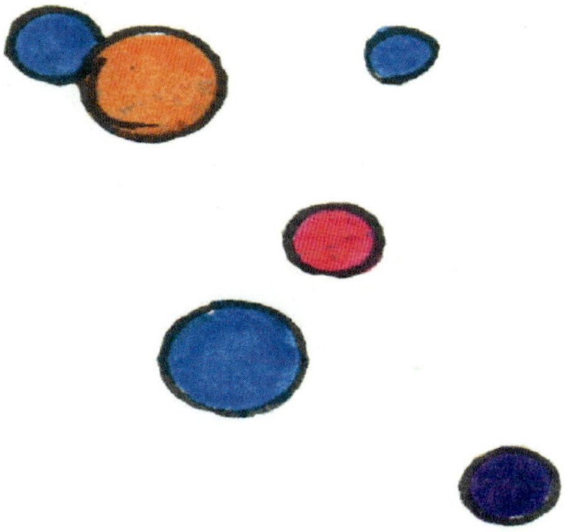

I would like to dedicate this book to the students of the Frederick Law Olmsted School in Buffalo, New York, and to my friends and family who never stopped believing in me, especially Robbie. Thank you for your support.

The Adventures of Jasper

Copyright© 2013 by Roselyn Kasmire

All rights reserved. No part of this publication may be reproduced or transmitted in any form or by any means, electronic or mechanical, including photocopy, recording, or any information storage and retrieval system, without permission in writing from the publisher.

Requests for permission to make copies of any part of the work should be submitted online at info@mascotbooks.com or mailed to Mascot Books, 560 Herndon Parkway #120, Herndon, VA 20170.

PRT1013A

Printed in the United States

Library of Congress Control Number: 2013945341

ISBN-13: 9781620864180
ISBN-10: 1620864185

www.mascotbooks.com

The Adventures of JASPER

Roselyn Kasmire

Illustrated by Blair Rusin

One day, Jasper came home with two truckloads of candy. He told his mom he won an award for eating the most candy in school.

Mom said, "That candy is not good for you. You should throw it all away!"

But he didn't feel the same way as Mom. Jasper loved candy.

Mom asked Jasper to get ready for bed. He jumped into bed, but he didn't brush his teeth. Instead, Jasper put on his pajamas and ate another piece of chocolate.

He gazed upon the mountain of wrappers next to his bed and had a strange bubbly feeling in his tummy as he fell asleep.

Jasper woke up to find himself in a mystical world full of goodies. He spotted something from the corner of his eye. It was a huge chocolate bird!

"Yummy!" he said, and tried to get closer to it.

As he approached the bird, he reached for a chocolate feather but the bird spotted him and said, "You'll be sorry!" and flew away.

He looked up as the bird flew away and noticed a bubblegum tree. *Where did the bird fly to?* wondered Jasper.

He thought he was dreaming so he pinched himself. "Ouch! That hurt! Maybe this isn't a dream," he said. He decided to keep exploring this new world.

Jasper stopped suddenly because he saw a huge purple pond full of soda! He jumped in and started to drink until the pond was gone.

Suddenly, a big yellow fruit appeared. It was a banana. The banana turned to Jasper and said, "Hello. Who are you?"

"My name is Jasper and I'm lost," he replied.

"Hello, Jasper. My name is Bobby Banana. What are you doing?"

"I was drinking all the soda in this pond," said Jasper.

"Well, you shouldn't have done that. You'll get sick," replied Bobby Banana.

Jasper snapped back, "You sound like my mother."

"I was just trying to help. No need to be rude," replied Bobby Banana.

"I'm sorry to snap at you, but I'm lost and confused. I don't know where I am."

"You are in between two towns. Junkietown is on the right and Healthyville is on the left. You can go to either town you like," Bobby Banana explained.

“Thank you, Bobby Banana. I love chocolate so I know exactly where I’m going,” said Jasper. Jasper ran as fast as he could until he saw a sign that said, “Welcome to Junkietown”.

Jasper stopped in his tracks in shock. He was right in front of a giant donut with juicy jelly coming out of its sides.

"Hello, young man. How are you? My name is Jerry Jelly Bun," said the donut.

"Can you tell me where I can find some chocolate?" asked Jasper.

"I can tell that you are not from around here," said Jerry Jelly Bun.

Jasper asked, "Is it that obvious?"

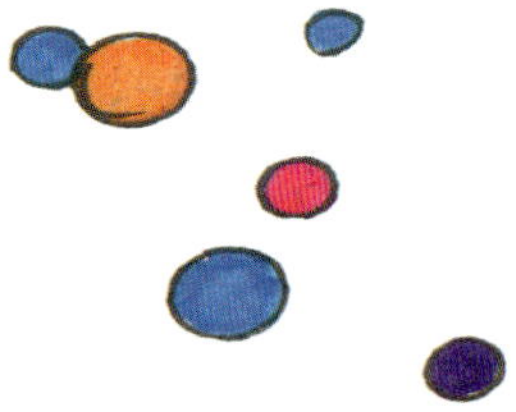

"You should keep going down the road until you hit Maple Syrup Street. You'll see a house made of chocolate waffles. Knock on the door and ask for Charlie Chocolate Bar," said Jerry Jelly Bun.

"Well thank you very much, Jerry Jelly Bun," Jasper replied.

Once he arrived, Jasper stopped and admired the chocolate waffle house. As he looked at it, he was tempted to take a bite, but he heard voices and decided to push the marshmallow doorbell.

All of a sudden, the door opened and a huge bar of chocolate asked, "How may I help you?"

Jasper asked, "Are you Charlie Chocolate Bar?"

"Why yes I am," said Charlie Chocolate Bar.

"Can I eat your house? It looks so yummy," said Jasper.

"No way, boy! I have a playground in my yard made out of peanut butter cups that you can eat instead," replied Charlie Chocolate Bar.

"Thank you so much," Jasper said. He went around the backyard to see the playground. He thought to himself, *Wow! This looks awesome.* Jasper kept eating and eating.

After stuffing his belly, Jasper felt sick. He became so fat that he had to roll around to get to places. When Jasper saw the bird again, it said, "I told you that you'd be sorry."

"Thanks for the warning. I should have listened to you. I feel so sick and weak, I'm going to Healthyville," said Jasper.

After a long journey, he saw the sign that read, "Welcome to Healthyville".

Jasper spotted Bobby Banana in the distance. He rolled as fast as he could and screamed in despair, "I want my old body back!"

Bobby Banana calmed him down and said, "Everything will be okay."

Aaron Artichoke and Emily Eggplant came out to help Jasper, too. They gave Jasper a gold platter full of fruits and veggies.

"Thank you for your help," said Jasper. He picked up the gold plate and started eating the fruits and vegetables right away. Gradually, his strength returned and his waistline began to shrink.

Bobby Banana noticed that Jasper's body was transforming back to normal. He knew that meant his job was done. Bobby Banana led Jasper to a huge celery slide and pointed to the steps made of carrot sticks. Jasper climbed the carrot sticks and made his way to the top of the celery slide. Before sliding down, he waved to his new friends and called out a heartfelt thank you to them.

Jasper went down the slide and...

...landed in a pile of dirty clothes in his room.

From downstairs, Mom heard a big thump and ran up to check on Jasper.
"Are you okay?" his mom called.

Jasper picked up the candy in his room and gave it to his mom. "Let's just say that junkie foods are okay once in a while, but healthy foods are good all of the time," said Jasper.

Mom only nodded and smiled.

After clearing out all the junkie foods in his room, Jasper felt something in his pocket. It was a small box of raisins. There was a note on the box from Bobby Banana. It read, "Fruit is nature's candy."

THE
END

My Favorite Fruit is

____

My Favorite Vegetable is

____

Roselyn's Favorite Candy is

Swedish Fish.

Her Favorite Fruit is

Strawberries.

Her Favorite Vegetable is

Brussels Sprouts.

Author Roselyn Kasmire holds a Master's Degree in Special Education from Buffalo State College and has worked as a public school teacher for nine years. She is dedicated to community outreach and the education of young minds. Roselyn's books seek to entertain, educate, and give children a positive framework for proper development.

For more information about Roselyn's books and teaching plans, please visit www.roselynkasmire.com.

To Xander !! :)

Make sure you eat your veggies! ♡ xoxo
always
[illegible]